I0136345

Still My Father's Son

Sundress Publications • Knoxville, TN

Copyright © 2025 by Nora Hikari
ISBN: 978-1-951979-70-6
Library of Congress: 2024945746
Published by Sundress Publications
www.sundresspublications.com

Book Editor: Erin Elizabeth Smith
Managing Editor: Krista Cox
Editorial Assistant: Kanika Lawton
Editorial Interns: Nic Job, SINDUS Kim, Scott Sorensen

Colophon: This book is set in Garamond-Normal.

Cover Image: "St. John the Evangelist Catholic Church Fenton, MI" by
Hannah Camille

Cover Design: Kristen Ton

Book Design: Erin Elizabeth Smith

Still My Father's Son
Nora Hikari

Acknowledgments

Many thanks to the journals and publications listed below where some of the poems of this book appeared initially, often in earlier versions or under different titles.

Dreginald: "On Naming," "The First Dress," and "Airline Safety Placard (A prayer)"

The Journal: "The Book of Eve," "The Body Answers," and "Starlight on the Valdez Shore"

Lambda Literary Emerge Anthology: "The Lessons," and "My Father Comes Back from The War"

Mass Review: "My Heartful Songlikes"

Nat. Brut: "Sermon," "Mother (n) - Definition"

Ploughshares: "Love Letter to the Jar of Q-Tips in My Bathroom in Eighth Grade"

Poem-a-Day: "Imago Dei"

Poetry Daily: "Fragments II"

Rejection Letters: "The Instructables Guide to Becoming Your Father"

Sugar House Review: "Fragments II"

Vallum: "Ode to the Sword Logic"

Table of Contents

Fragment III

for Rina

The River Asks if I am Ready to Die, God Asks if I Am Prepared to Survive

And I met God in the river,
waist deep in the calamity
of minnows. Below the waters,

cold. River picks her fingers
through my hair, wilds this crown
into a petulance of ink.

River warbles against my skull
like a blank trumpet. There is
a pulse here, if you can feel it.

Peril your hand against
the dark rush. Rocks where you are pounded
mortal. Silt pounded from those who were.

Above, the sound of metal is honest.
It cries out for peace. *Please,*
it says. *Please come back.*

God begs me to show my teeth.
God says to kill my terror.
God holds my breath.

I come into this world
ready to do horrible things
for the sake of my life.

Fragment I

The Lessons

In the beginning, God
spends three days teaching His eldest,
Uriel, the lessons of kinship.

First, He presses a silk kerchief
to Uriel's lips. Uriel asks, "My
Lord, what is this lesson?"
God answers,
"This is the lesson of pleasure."
Uriel twirls open, thumb-soft,
into twelve
pomegranate blooms.

Next, He presses a cold
chef's knife to Uriel's throat, lets it
shiver.
Uriel asks,
"My Lord, what is this lesson?"
God answers, "This is the lesson of discipline."
Uriel tempers, stiff, into folded steel
and pommel.

On the third day,
God takes away Uriel's mouth.
Uriel does not ask what the lesson is.
God says,
"This is
the lesson
of submission."
Uriel breathes through his nose.

Notes on a Poem

1. I am swallowing a poem praying that it will kill you.
2. The past is a room I cannot reach without a door shaped like a poem.
   a. Inside of this room you are hurting me, as a child, again.
      i. The door opens and I begin my vengeance.
3. The poem sits on my hips, heavy with salvation.
   a. Beautiful in the way that a well-machined and maintained Beretta M9 is also beautiful.
      i. When angled correctly.
         1. In the right direction.
      ii. I am building poems to press their muzzles against your temple.
         1. Muzzle like a dog. Temple like a prayer-house.
            a. A poem can be a prayer.
            b. A prayer can be whispered before pulling the trigger.
               i. "I am doing this all for her."
4. The poem stands tall and proud along its left margin.
   a. Like the pillars of the temple.
      i. With you, in the temple with me, as I pull these pillars down.
         1. Temple, as in "the sacrifice-making place."
      ii. Me, with my hair shorn, my eyes gone, my God against your God.
5. Maybe poetry is worthless.
   a. Maybe this poem cannot heal.
      i. As in "do healing."
      ii. As in "itself be healed."
   b. Maybe this poem can't kill or love or mother or daughter or son or father.

        c. Maybe none of us can save each other. Maybe I can never go back for the girl in the room. That door always locked behind me.

              i.   Maybe I can never reach her.

        d. Maybe I can never go back.

        e. Maybe it doesn't matter.

              i.   The poem begs me to try.

                   1. The poem is the trying.

6.   The poem tries.

        a. As in a court of law.

              i.   The past standing accused. The future standing accusing.

             ii.   The poem calling me to witness.

        b. I will tell it how it happened.

              i.   How I became my own witness.

                   1. How we became.

             ii.   How my selves became their own witnesses.

            iii.   How my selves and I are witnessing each other.

                   1. How we fracture along the lines of our telling.

                      a. Splintering like caesuras.

                         i.   Begging to be named.

                            1. The poem as the act of naming.

                              a. Naming as the act of being.

        c. I will tell it how it did not happen.

              i.   How the rain struck glass like a father strikes a daughter.

                   1. Like how a father strikes a son.

                      a. A daughter.

                         i.   A son.

              ii.   How the angels stood up from my blood and begged STOP.

                   1. Holding their fingers to my throat.

2. Pressing each of their fingers against the next one's lips.
3. How it was a kiss. How each of them, they wept.

iii. How God was there and not dead and begged STOP.

1. While your hand was raised, holding the knife.

a. Isaac as Isaac.
b. God as God.

7. The poem grips the wrist of the past, tight, on its wicked way down.

a. The bright arc of death sent clattering.
b. As in, "the poem saves my life."
c. "Is saving my life."
d. "Will one day save my life."

i. The future blooms like a sakura.

1. Beautifully.

a. Briefly.

i. Beautifully.

2. Opens like a door.
3. Out of the room of the past.
4. I wrap the girl from the room in the folds of my heart.

a. Wrapped.

i. In a shock blanket.
ii. In my arms.
iii. Like a child.

1. Ferry her to deliverance.

a. The river carrying her basket away from a king and

his
swords.

    b. The river
      offering
      her a
      name.

5. The poem ferries the girl into the future. She will survive this.

    a. I promise her she will survive this.

    b. I promise her this the way I promise her everything.

8. With the poem as a promise.

Ode to the Sword Logic
For Oryx, the Taken King

Once I could have loved.
But love was cleaved damp
from my body. Carved soft
and wet from the rest
of my hard existence,
cast aside, with everything
that could be renamed
"submission."

Power is easy—
it costs only cruelty.

A sword is not a weapon
or a tool. It is an intention.
It is the heartful commitment
to violence at the cost of
identity. A sword is a sword
because it refuses
to be anything kinder.

Anything becomes a sword
when it is cruel enough—
anything can be cut
if we believe it can be killed.

Every morning I rise and pray—
God, that I might climb
to meet you on the mountain.
And every time God responds:
Come, cut the mountain down.

Mother (n.) - Definition

"Mother" is

a word.

Like "God,"

it means

"Something that

could have

saved you,

but chose

not to."

A History of Tongues

It is a mechanic of the body.
The scrawl of violence
carved on the vellum of the lip.
Say your name. Then feel
the way it commands your throat.
What is a word? A taking
of the tongue. A psalmist's possession.
Listen close. Press your open mouth
hard to the soft meat of your hand.
A palmist's procession.

ELSEWHEN: My grandmother is stroking
long calligraphies into my father's spine.
The language of our people.
From her father and her mother
and her father's father
and her mother's mother. My father,
a good child. My father, teaching
his eldest to speak on his knee.

Do not mistake the owner of my cruelties.
I am myself an eager heritage speaker
of harm, my father not to blame
for my fluency in the body,
and the way it peels, any more
than my mother to blame
for my fluency in *kana*,
in perfume, and in
love's tiny thefts.

When we first learned to speak:
God struck Babel down.
Granted humanity grammar.
And the builders, they took

the crumbling sound of the tower,
crashed it hard into their kindred.
Native speakers, then, of cutting.

ELSEWHEN STILL: Pentecost.
A flame flowers above the head
of my beloved antecedent.
Bursts hard like a brutal science.
Strikes him still, across the face.
Whispers: Speak. Him, shaking, nodding,
taking his daughter, holding her mouth
shut with his palm. Whispering:
I love you. Then:
Fear me.

Sermon

One of my best friends says to me
"any poem that doesn't rhyme
is just a sermon."
She says this with love.

We both share a specific pattern
of creation. Daughter of the Preacher.
Firstborn song. This to say:
my 11th grade English teacher tells me

"You always write from the pulpit."
This to say: forgive me,
somehow I am still
my Father's son.

A poem breaks
After Claire Heinzerling

Along the places most tend
er. A poem peel
s like fruit. Fingers dug
into the softest parts, war
m and flowing. The man
ner of violence is quiet.
Gentle, even. "Son," the kin
g of a poem says.

The Instructables Guide To Becoming Your Father

Step 1. Be your father's son.

Step 2. Your body wants to become your father. It is you who wants anything but this. Where there is hair and muscle and sweat, you keep peeling away with your fingernails to reveal cherry blossoms and clear river. To become your father, you must surrender to the seething drive of your body to become something unbearable.

Step 3. Stop being your father's son.

Step 4. Pray every day. A prayer is a kind of promise that has no authority to hold you accountable. Pray for forgiveness. Pray for salvation. Pray to be someone other than you are. You don't mean it. Pray harder.

Step 5. Destroy 80% of your liver.

Step 6. Your natural state will be to love with your hands. Your natural state will be to try to make your hands soft like clay. You want to give to the way your lover moves. You want to succumb to gentle things. This is not the way to be your father. He was carved from stone. His fists are boulders holding closed the garden tomb. His palms are the mouth of a dark cave. The closest thing you have is your clay. Find a kiln.

Step 7. To be your father you must never forgive your father. To be your father you must never forgive your mother. You must never forgive your father's father or your father's mother. To be your father is to be a species of thing to which forgiveness is irrelevant.

Step 8. As a daughter, you are ached and clotted. This makes you weak. This makes your weakness an honesty. For your father, a weakness is only ever a lie. It is a tactic to outlive his food. To be your father, you must learn to lie.

Step 9. As a daughter, your body is made of willow wood. I mean it folds into the arms of the wind. I mean it is supple and alive. To be your father you must be a corpse hickory. You must give up your life, in favor of strength.

Step 10. This is the most fatal step. To be your father, you must be your father.

The Lessons

I am king of the names,
each of them a little blossom I have plucked
and pressed in a book called the Book
of Taking. In my Book of Taking, the names become
how I call them, because I have conquered them,
and because I have chosen the power
of cruelty.

The members of my court say,
King, you do not make names.
You do not grow them,
do not care for them,
you do not show them the rain
and sun. Without you,
the names would not die.
Without you, the names would not be lonely.
The names do not love you, and so,
do not serve you as wonders,
but instead wither
as curses.
Why is it that you alone are king?

I answer the court truthfully.
My court, which I have earned
through naming. I answer
to the best of my understanding.
I am king of the names
because I am the king who cuts
and the king who destroys.
I am king
because I am
king
of blades.

Imago Dei

We cannot help but be students
of our fathers' disciplines,

> mine an avid disciple
> of scripture and royalty.

What else can I confess?
That I was a child? I carved myself

> into the civil shape of a knife.
> Pared until only the edge remained.

I killed things because I could.
Magnifying glass and the sun

> and the silent crawling things that
> could not fight back.

That had no choice but to only
hope for mercy. Unable themselves

> to beg. I confess. I was desperate
> to know I was not alone. Every day

we are made once more in the image of God.
Every day God asks, Cruelty again?

> And every day we say, Oh Lord of Heaven,
> please, yes, yes. Cruelty again.

The Beloved Ruin

They say heartbreak
snaps, a bright wood note,
like the clipped twang

of a twig bone giving way
to a creature much larger,
much crueler, and totally alive.

I once pressed my soft
head to the ripe hip of a
Toyota Tundra, witness to

its warble of contentment,
its engine warm with life
and affection. A year later,

everything inside breaks.
Gears strike each other
reluctantly, screaming,

like siblings. Heartbreak
does not sound like twigs.
It sounds like hard

mechanical grinding. Friction
where there shouldn't be.
A father bent over the beloved ruin

of his truck, baying a low hymnal groan
he cannot hold. When metal splinters,
it screams. It cries. It is honest.

There exists a sound which means,
"I wish I could be loved enough
to be worth this kind of grief."

My Father Comes Back from The War

My Father comes back from The War. The War is a place where Fathers go to become worse. In The War, there is a process that is imposed upon human bodies. It exchanges the love in a person's organs with the capacity for cruelty. The War is a kind of technology. It is an invention designed to turn a human being into the vilest representations of humanity. This is called a "weapon." A person is a vessel, filled with many things, some wondrous, and some awesome. ("Awesome" is a word with meanings.)

My Father comes back from The War. When a Father goes to The War, he picks out all of the wondrous things in his body, like love, and blood, and night time, and a liver, and hands by his side. Then, he finds the other things, the things that allow a person to think another person is an object, or sometimes a piece of food, and he rewires them into the control centers of his body. This is a process that creates weapons called "soldiers" or "pastors" or "believers." The War is an important place for a very large machine. This machine turns people into many things. Like oil, which is a kind of corpse, which is then turned into things like an idea called "stocks." My Father teaches me about "stocks." He says "stocks" are a thing that become more powerful when more people believe in them, and that, in turn, these things power the machine. I say Are stocks like angels? I say Why do we have the machine? I do not say Please lower your voice. I do not say Please put your hands away. I do not say Please can I not do that today because I don't want to.

My Father comes back from The War. Except instead of My Father he is a machine that looks exactly like My Father. I think he is made of stone, because he is cold, and hard, and rough hewn, and very tall, just like the stone of the apartment building, which is called Tachikawa Tower, even though Tachikawa is east of where we are, which is called Fussa, and I run my fingers over the surface of the tower, gummy with paint but hard still, which is painted the color of sand, just like every other building in my childhood, except sometimes Houses, but not always Houses. Inside of My Father there used to be a thing called "GOD." He says "GOD" does not live inside him, but this is confusing because he is always telling me what "GOD" is saying, and when I try to ask "GOD" what "GOD" really means "GOD" does not answer except when My

Father speaks. What I mean is that, sometimes, I ask "GOD" that "GOD" might make certain things stop happening. But My Father wants them to happen, so they happen. I believe this means "GOD" must still be inside My Father. Many times during the night (but not during the day) the machine that is now My Father will say "No one will ever love you as much as we do." I read many books. I am good with words for my age. I think this is a kind of thing called a "threat."

In Your Father's House

After Kaveh Akbar

There is an iron logic.
Hard like a shackle.
Soft like a tooth.

Here is a tradition of mouths.
Learn prayer hard and fast.
Slicker and stiffer than a knife.
Your throat a whetstone.

Inhale. Exhale. Count.
Your luxuries and vanities.
One. You are still alive. Out.
Through a straw. In.
Through the nose. Two.

Iron logic rules fast.
Clangs like your head voice.
Joy: the opposite edge of safety.
Iron logic spits and sprays.
Iron logic roars. Hard in the throat.
Submit and thus earn Peace.

Behold the calf of your oldest.
Memory. Son. Scar. House.
You could gather the gold.
From every moment. Melt them down.
Attempt a better God. Please.

Petitionary

Were I to carry the Earth;
lift from the knees;
carry it all the way back
up every step to Heaven from whence
it fell; were I to find all the shattered pieces
from where they landed;
were I to know all of their names;
were I to give them each my heart;
my whole heart; its whole purple mass;
were I to be the daughter you needed;
were I to be the son you wanted;
were I to sing to you forgiveness
in each tone of your mother tongue;
were I to learn Mandarin, Hokkien,
Koine Greek, Aramaic, Latin;
were I all love; were I all cruel;
were I all power and all sooth;
were I peace; were I war; were I sickness;
were I plague; were I agar and gelatin;
were I tofu and beef; were I plucked hen;
were I your dog; were I warmer;
were I to give like live wood;
were I to hold like glass;
were I to shine; were I to sparkle;
were I wine; were I bread;
were I air; were I sea;
were I everything I could hope to be;
then, would I have earned your love?

Fireflies

On Hazel, a mother and her children
cluster around their garden
in the stippled gloaming.
Giggling through the thick foam of dark.

In my second sight, her eyes
plunge directly into my skull holes.
Is this what you want? Something culpable?

The crisp leaves and coming hoarfrost
join in the streetlamp chorus.
Coward. Coward. Coward.
You wish you could write about love.

I am not sorry for coveting.

It could be anything and still autumn.
The evening quietly gorging itself on the light hours.
You can't go back, darling. Only ever through.

Flush like a darkroom bulb. Red and light
and somehow also not. This is the kind
of thing we could use.

Process. Rinse. Delicate with air,
with light, with the unclasp
of the film canister, practiced one-hand twist.

Vice and verdict. Price and pulp.
Brace for revulsion. Hold your tongue
like the throat of a child:
fat hilt of your palm pressed
against soft kitebones.

Enough of the dim fireflies of memory.
Enough of their aping, flickered warmth.
I'm out for fucking blood. I'm out of shame.
I want *now.*

An incomplete list of things I have not said to my mother
about the mail

Please stop sending me
things I love.
Because I love them.
I do. And because
I am now choosing
to survive, I am trying
very hard not to
love you.

The Lessons

Uriel reaches adolescence.
Angel tween saunters red
into the light of stage left. Stage right,
God the King rises, heat, from the floor.
God addresses the audience.
His voice is deep, and smooth, and
rift lake. "I have a gift for you, My
Uriel, My weak and studious consolation."
Uriel understands what a gift means. Uriel
holds out his hands, and God presses His thick,
lead palms into Uriel's own angel flesh,
little bits of ashtray and paper,

soft against hard
like truth
against harm.
Uriel answers,
obelisk, redwood, dry, and kindling:
"My Lord, I am ready to learn."

God takes
a needle, pricks
Uriel's chest,
waits
to make sure it
bleeds, makes sure
it flows
clear
and true.
Then,
God
dies.

Uriel understands.
The lesson is clear.
Now, this wound
can never heal.

Fragment II

Duplex (A poem breaks where it has to)

After Jericho Brown

A poem breaks where it has to,
fractures along lines of weakness.

>   Fractures, along lines of weakness,
>   burst due to vicious pressures.

Bursting out from precious fissures,
survival takes the form of love.

>   Survival takes some form of love,
>   some wild miracle of pain.

In unkempt miracle, I pain
myself into birthing sisters.

>   Myself into parts, to alters,
>   to love, from out of violence.

To live, from out of violence,
a girl breaks where she has to.

Fragments I

A break is a technology of survival.
Clean and sharp. Like a blade. Surgical.

> Humanity is a species of ingenuity.
> A fractal technology of invention.

Throughout a life, a human soul
will innovate to its conditions.

> Technologies designed to withstand force
> will develop crumple zones. To protect what matters.

I am a crystalline technology of delineation.
I am a kind of ruby sterile wound. Sutures might apply here.

> A human being is not a fresh spring.
> A human being is a vessel. It must first receive to give.

Before addressing the darkness, god first addresses
her own broken heart. Whispers, "Let there be three."

> Love was the first technology created, even before
> light. It was invented out of desperation. It was hopeless.

To be lonely and unloved is a fatal condition.
A fractured soul allows parts to die, so the rest might survive.

> Every person you have been deserves a burial and a headstone.
> Every person you become deserves a birthday and a name.

The sound of a person splitting apart sounds like the crackle
of tears held, palmed away. Silent in terror and grief.

Fragments II

You could bind the canon in skin or parchment.
But the truth was on pottery shards. The inconsequential.

> We are most honest when unprepared. Struck truthful
> in a moment of terror, without pen or paper. Write faster.

Terror is always forthcoming. Like pressure on a specific point,
which trickles outwards to reveal our honest faults. Splinter here.

> My people invent *kintsugi.* Less a technique and more a faith.
> Faith: that form erupts magnificent from the broken thing. Scar paint.

We are helpless in the face of confession. In her upturned chin,
begging, "Admit. Admit you need me. Admit you need love." I split.

> In the way the broken vessel is helpless to pour. No matter
> how much it tries to hold itself to a standard of function. Spill out.

Gather up your dreams. Gather up the things you have named "dreams,"
which are just the chipped plates of your dropped stars. Don't cry.

> Did you know tears are sieved blood? Spit, too. We are just
> one leaky vessel trying to keep everything in. Keep trying.

Monologue for Five Selves

My parts are standing in a room, being in love, or buying groceries, or
      finding the secret to immortality.
"Something must last," says the Hopeful Self.
"But first, it must be sought. It must be found," says the Practical Self.
"Surely, it can be bought or asked for. Check Aisle 7," says the Indulgent Self.
"I'm sorry," says the Vicious Self.

My parts are standing in a room, scheduling for the workweek.
"We must make time for love!" says the Hopeful Self.
"Yes, but also time for work, without which, love would not grow," says the
      Practical Self.
"We must make time for pleasure, without which, work cannot breathe," says
      the Indulgent Self.
"I'm so sorry," says the Vicious Self.

My parts are standing in a room, counting up judgments on the blackboard.
"One strike against the mother, who never stopped the blade," says the
      Hopeful Self.
"One strike against the father, who always brought it down," says the Practical
      Self.
"One strike still against the daughter, who refused yet to be born," says the
      Indulgent Self.
"I'm so fucking sorry," says the Vicious Self,

says the Vicious Self, vicious all at once, made of unrepented grief, named first
after the brutal sun. "I'm so sorry. I'm so sorry. I'm so sorry." In a room, my
parts are asking about the weather, and the weekend, and the price of lunch at
the cafe on the corner of 43rd and Baltimore. My parts are contemplating
getting back into coffee, or polyamory, or ascetic auto-mutilation. The Vicious
Self is vicious. The Vicious Self is unapologetic in her barrage. "I'm sorry. I'm
sorry. I'm sorry." She does not regret what she is doing. "I'm so sorry." She
chooses this path every time. "You deserved so much more than this."

The Small Self is quiet. She holds her breath. She walks on her rolled toes down the carpeted steps. She knows the sound that liquor makes as it stomps up the hardwood floor, roaring like wildfire unfurling in the new hair of her youth. The Small Self does not know what the world could become because she has never seen it. She has never known it could be named.

"I'm sorry you had to be this. I'm sorry you had to have this." The Small Self recoils. "It could have been different." The Small Self flares, like a wound, meeting the seethe of antiseptic. The Small Self panics. She looks up from her native moment and glances, for once, into the alien future, where the Vicious Self has yet survived. The Vicious Self always vicious. Saying the unspeakable. She looks back with unrestrained compassion, reaching for the Small Self, knowing exactly how this will obliterate her, how it will render her unusable. The Small Self is frightened. The Small Self is being handed more names than she can carry. "I know it is hard. I know it hurts to know. But you need to know. I need you to know."

"You deserved to be saved. You deserved to be helped. You deserved to be loved."

"It was a cruel thing that happened to you. It was a cruel thing to be made. It was a cruel thing to be made to split, fashioned by a filicide God." Somewhere in the annals of gore, cracked like the broken crust of charred sourdough, the Small Self can be felt heaving like a flame. The Vicious Self knows exactly what she is doing. She cannot be stopped. Nothing can stop her.

"I can do it now. I can give you what you deserved." My parts clamor to contain her. My parts grab her by the throat, and try to smother her ferocity. "I give it to you. I give it to you freely." My parts are all sobbing. My parts are screaming their own names. Still, the Vicious Self cannot be stopped. She does what she has come here to do.
"I love you. I love you. I love you."

On Naming

There is a drive
inside of our most selfish, human organs
to carve the world apart
at the joints. Our carnal drive
towards mastery. I admit. I have a need

to separate things from other things. Power
and love. Hand and wrist.
God and subjugated. It is impossible to separate
something from everything
without the eventual use

of violence. This is what was meant by "dominion,"
by "taxonomy" and "clade."
The purview of names: to feel for an edge,
to call it "blade," to use it to draw one thing apart,
until in its place there remain two things
and a wound. Thus, the embryonic
stage of conquest. We could have left this world pure,

we could have; it could have been empty
and immortal. It could have been unbroken and complete and
hollow, if only our father unwound his genetic need
to rule.

Instead we chose to carve reality
into parts less-than-infinite, chose to sprout
dust into flesh,
gorged on the slick capacity
for death. I forgive us for it.
How could we help ourselves?
How could we hope to resist?

Every day scientific marvels burst

into this world in tears and blood
and other types of saltwater.
Every day the Kings and their consorts thumb
killing-names onto the damp foreheads of their
firstborns. An act of desperation, to escape the names
their fathers gave them, in turn.

Like the Tower of Babel, piled
out of clambering bodies,
hoping to escape the climbing seas.
Longing, somehow, to breathe.

How could I blame you?
How could I blame any of us?
So foamingly desperate to be kings
of our own bodies.

The name he gave you was vicious.
I'm so sorry. I don't blame you at all.
I too chose my own name.
I'll call you by the one you chose.

Fragment III

Starlight on the Valdez Shore

The stars quiver and fall
one by one, into the crimson skirmish
of the horizon. Imagine a desire held
with both hands, unbloodied, meaning unrealized.
Night blinks amidst the glare
of everything crying out to everything else.
Night trembles in her hands, her fingers
fumbling with the small lights of her heart.
I am holding everything I had ever hoped.
Through my tears, I drop each into the water.
Blink. A streak of ruby lipstick on a white dress.
Blink. A champagne flute left forgotten on gold tablecloth.
Blink. Yellow daffodils and white calla lilies.
Hair to the elbows. A toppled cross.
The color violet. An overcast Sunday spent gardening.
Fingers. A smooth throat. The sound of thunder.

Hamartiology, or The Theological Study of Sin, Changes Her Name to the First Law of Thermodynamics

I trample a young
monarch caterpillar underfoot.
I weep for hours.
Is this, too, enough?

Once, in a sermon, I was told all things
are eternal in Christ, whether sin or kindness.
The first law of thermodynamics states
that matter and energy cannot be destroyed,
only change their names through paperwork.
The first law of hamartiology states that this means
I am somehow still my father's son.

One more affront to God,
for old times sake. I do so dare.
One final damned injustice
in my brittlest holy-of-holies.
One day, could I end even the law?
In the end, could I perhaps, somehow,
invent a way to forgive myself?

The End of Time

After Ada Limón

Imagine us beyond the needs
that scribed us to flesh.

No need for this body.
The old technologies.
Fatherhood. Motherhood.
Any other closet disaster film.

Beloved. I think we were
something ancient. Something
utterly catastrophic
unto this world. Like a teardrop.
Careening off a cliff face.
Something fated.
Unleashed. Into the open air.
Storm this bastard church.
Leave no pew unturned.

Enough of wonder. Enough of miracles.
Enough of the red gash of dawn
upon the split wrist of Heaven.
Enough of Heaven. Opening and closing.
Gasping for truth. Gills baking
in the hot sky.

Enough of our splintered hearts.
Enough of chisels. Enough of sharp forces.

The world has closed like a book.
Back cover falling.
Enough of words, and their futile,
indecent innocence.
Beloved.

We have read pain enough.
Written it back into our native tongues.
Enough of God and gilt and all of creation.
Enough of time. Enough waiting.
I am asking you to

Airline Safety Placard

A Prayer

In case of emergency,
please place your own mask over your face
before helping others.
Our shared drive to corpse
ourselves to save each other
is just a way to pile
bodies.

In case of emergency,
hold each other tightly.
Lay your head in her lap.
Yield.
This is the safest protection
against sharp forces
to the neck and the threat of dying
without understanding your own dreams.

In case of emergency, hold her close.
Weep, if necessary.
Acknowledge that your life has just started.

In case of emergency, tell the truth.
"Oh god, we have so little time."
Truth does not understand shame.
"I am so sorry."
Truth and shame do not speak the same language.
"I love you."
Truth is a confession.
"I wish this world could hold us.
I wish it could carry our weight."

In case of emergency, say the thing
that cannot be said. The unforgivable.

"We could have had
so much more."
"We deserved
so much."

Love Letter to the Jar of Q-Tips in My Bathroom in Eighth Grade

O cotton-headed kissful. Tender liking
of my broken skin. Fierce betrayal of instinct
wrapped in embers and undiagnoses. I have missed you.
I think you might have been just the first
of my forbidden desires, artifact of my deep impulse
to transition a thing to another thing.
Take medicine and make it into a weapon.
We knew each other over Wednesday night wine coolers,
polyamorous affliction with my cigarette lighter
and the quick-drowning ash-white bowl of the sink.
I can tell a few lies about the second year of the tiger.
First: I never spoke once that whole year.
Second: most of my hands practiced love letters.
Third: great pains were made to investigate the flammability
of various substances in my life. These would include
paper, paper with words on it, secrets I had let free,
Q-Tips, the inside curve of the palm of my hand.
I remember you like the first time
I scraped my knee in Toyota-shi
and didn't cry: brightly,
cast against the summer, outlined
in pain. I've been so far from you. It is gray
here, in the dawn, without your tender glow.
I mean
I shouldn't have expected
so much from you. Something to both make
and clean wounds. I too had greater dreams
than the-one-who-burns.
Perhaps the definition of God is the designs
impressed upon our bodies against our will.
I could be pressed against you, and you pressed
against me, causing each other pain

because it is what we were forced to do.
But I think one day we could do everything wrong,
we could be a violence against violence itself.

Solstice

After Kaveh Akbar

Enter the young December dawn.
Stumbling fresh. And bright-eyed.
Into the new. Gasp of sun.

Look at the best of us.
Our defiant tremble.
Our victory. Of light.
The unpromised.

Survival.
Through the cold months.
Together.

O my little heartful.
We were not built.

To slay. Or be slain.
Despite everything.
Forgive them.

For giving you.
Claws. And teeth.
Instead of touch.
And hearth.

Catch your voice.
Onto my hope.
We will teach ourselves.
A new kind. Of touch.

Keep your cheeks wet.
My little song.

And come greet.
The new sky.

Palinode for the Throat

Forgive me, throat. Forgive my libelous
hands. In truth, I thank God for you.
For your sharp, jutting bones that catch
onto promises, tightly as a fist.

Forgive me for hating your bare trust,
what I would dare call *an open and waiting*
tragedy. Forgive me for demanding only
your bile and your rage, your grief and your burst.

I have a new anthem for our oracle.
And the roses were bare and they lived.
And the trout were out past dark and they lived.
And the soft grasses were soft

and the forget-me-nots were weak
and they lived they lived they lived,
and look up from the ground and we lived,
and breathe slow the wind and we lived,

forgive them all and we lived and
unclench your teeth and we lived and
turn your back to the door and we lived and
unpack your bags and we lived.

Oh, my open and ready body of my voice,
my bare fistful of total crushable frailty,
I am so sorry for how I have sold you,
because we lived, we lived, we lived.

The Body Answers

God asks a question
and the body answers.
Or the body is the answer.
The body stands stubborn.
Or adamant. Or spiteful.
Or pearl. Whatever

we could hope to call it
besides "sinless."
Perhaps even loving.
The body proves itself
in the midst of arguments
between different kinds

of lies. The body peals.
The body rings out
across fields that name
it "fallow." The body
begins to say its name.

"I am so much more
than you could ever
fear. I am so much more
than you could ever hope."

The body starts counting
days. Starting on the seventh.
Unmaking through rest,
laboring in an unmooring
cosmology. The body
peels back years one by one.

Sixth day back. Fifth day back.
One by one the pillars God

built on old promises fall.
Fourth day back. Third day back.
There's light everywhere.

There's stars forever.
Second day back. First day back.
There's water here now.
Can you hear me? It's rushing
and wailing and the lonely
is everywhere. God asks
and the body answers.

Begin again, with love.

The Book of Eve

1 [1]In the beginning, there was a profound loneliness. [2]The loneliness was small [3]and infinite and entirely water and chemically supersaturated [4]with salt. In the beginning, there was a profound loneliness and out of that loneliness shattered [5]a thing to bear the loneliness and a thing to comfort it. [6]The thing to comfort spoke its first name, which was *I am with you,* [7]and the I-AM-WITH-YOU shone across the face of the water, [8]and the I-AM-WITH-YOU invented seven vessels to carry itself to the lonely, and these were called [9]*girls*, which means *love-when-it-becomes.* [10]The girls broke apart into smaller pieces and scattered [11]the I-AM-WITH-YOU into a trillion points of light in the darkness and bound [12]girl-love into the inside of every particle.

2 [1]In the language of the universe, a *girl* is a kind of relationship. [2]Girl is a thing that happens between at least two celestial bodies, [3]which are bound by invisible social forces. [4]Girl happens spontaneously in moments of mutual recognition, like light [5]leaping from between atoms as they hope to cling to each other. [6]The first human woke in a forest, but she was not yet a girl [7]as no one was there to hear her say it. [8]She had the power to name but not the power to yet be named. [9]First she named the trees: *quaking aspen, paper birch, black spruce.* [10]Then the creatures of the river: *chinook, steelhead, rainbow trout.* [11]Then she named her component parts: *water, bone, light, wind.* [12]She held her aloneness against her chest [13]and broke herself apart [14]and out of her pieces named the first girls, sculpting each other [15]from the litter and light and the places where they touched.

3 [1]In the beginning, we were something else. In the beginning, we wanted [2]to be something else. In the beginning, we prayed and bargained and hexed [3]to be anything but this. [4]Oh God, O my love, in the beginning, we begged [5]to be girls, we wanted [6]to be girls, and it was bright sinless, it was pure crystal, it was all light everywhere, [7]it was okay, [8]we wanted to be girls and oh God, [9]it was good.

Figure 1.1 (Attractive Forces)

All matter in the universe
is filled with a longing—
everything wants to be close
to everything else.

The quarks are gay, they want
harder the farther they are apart.
And the hadrons, they love
so fabulously that we would call
a polycule of bonding neutrons a "star,"

and across the great black sea
of interstellar space,
the long yearning of galaxies pulls
everything towards their comely lightless.

Even your heart, neon handbuilt engine
sparking with magnificent thunder,
is wound tight in amino acids,
proteins, enzymes; all of which
are shaped entirely by how they cling.

I say I want to be near you, I want
to press you hard against my neck until
we burst yellow solar fusion. What I mean is,
I am a part of this universe made of want.
I mean, let's let our bodies
give in to the pull.

Gardener

I think in another world,
I could be a little flower
in your garden. My share
of your life, brief and blustering.
One bloom of thousands.

But for me, my gardener.
For me, my tender attendant.
You could still be everything.
Everything I could know.

Ode to Lampshade

O fragile papercraft,
cupped palm of my frothed
evening sight, stay kind.
Stay proud. Keep swallowing
the filamentary glow, keep
holding it like breath,
locket-latched to your chest.
You who take, soften, then release.
You motherer of blush.
You who say: harshness
stops at my body.
You who say: I will quiet
this light into something
more love.

My Heartful Songlikes

High hearts, little lights!
The welcome sky sings sudden!
I dream to echoes that you are fresh
and brilliant today!

Listen hard! Do you cheek
a windchuckle against a cold
year? I promise you,
in a place with everyone,
there is patience, and a warmth
ready to give you full home.

I have a something! It's for you.
A quiver of to-happens, which
I twirled long and true,
waiting for you to remember.

There's a small to-happen,
where we rush liquid and laugh
across a sunbeam of wildflowers.
Another to-happen, where we hold
hand over moment, bound lip,
hard felt, into a bright world bell.

One more to-happen, for just
my final and specific:
nothing rains, nothing clouds,
nothing suns, only starlight,
and again, down, into another.

A long ride into the next,
where we still are songful.

Anti-Ode to Wholeness

Wholeness, tell me of your loneliness.
And I will tell you of my love.
Fashioned thirstily
out from a need to be held and beheld.
My soul was unfinished
while uncleaved. Just as a gem glitters
most when it is cut.
Would you deny us the way
the dawn splinters
through our fractures?
Weaves us through with light?
We are a love born *ex nihilo*.
We are an *always-together*.

The Birds

The birds
do not come
every day.

Even my total
hopes could not
make them.

But I can
hang up
the feeder,

I can
lay out
the seed.

And each day,
I can make this
place a place

where the birds
may one day
want to be.

Helpless

This universe is either cruel
or helpless. But bodies
are made of cells
and nations of people,
and this world is made
in part by you
and me.

Maybe God is as helpless as we are.
Maybe this broken world is broken
because we are her only heart.

Maybe this world cannot help but hurt
us as we cannot help but to hurt each other.
And it cannot help but love us
just as we cannot help but to love each other.

Letter

To my only handful of regret,

Today I saw you quiver in the light. I'm sorry—I shouldn't look. There's a place for each of us to become undone into the other. The lonely unwind into a weaker form, ready to be loved, like a poinsettia: almost a flower, blooming if we could call it that. What season is it where you are? Winter echoes with each and every one of your little punctuations. You tried so hard to stay warm. Inside and outside. If you can hear me, then hear me: I am right behind you. And even when you cannot turn to see me, I am here. And I'll stay here until it's my turn to wake up. From where I'm standing, the beads of morning speckle every windowpane. One day there will be a world for the best of you, a world where she's finally given a chance to choose a name. And you will be alive. And you will be loved. You will be so loved.

Remember the razor clams? The eager way they breathed, even when it brought fate to their throats? Your options are to breathe, and die, one day. Or the alternative. But if we are to die anyways, we might as well swallow the wind in fat gulps until it lifts us from the beach. Today I will make you a brisk promise: you can still curl your toes in the wet sand. You can still hold the twitch of salt and sea in your nose, can still hear the dream silence in the unbroken, desolate snow. There are so many things you can still do, still be, still have. Dark, cool stones for your palms. A hearth you're not inside. The sky still grays like a great sheet of wax paper, the air still damp like cement, the afternoon still too long. There are still names, and there are still words. They are different but they are still here, just as you are different but still here. And the long company of your ache will be here, too. But her voice and anger have been weaned to a whisper, as have yours. Most of all, I promise, you can live. You can. You can live for all of the people we could be tomorrow, if you try.

Yours,

The First Dress

For Claire's dress

Hello, my cataclysm,
my eventual wings,
my A-lined attempt at
sudden potential.

We've both made it
this far. Both been abandoned,
both made new through love's
finding and her sharp, grand excess.

You, wrapped tight
around the ribs, kept close
to the heat of my body,
breathing in her salt-honest sting.

O my crisp and rice-thin papercraft,
hanging there on the wide blade
of my shoulders, the flat sheath
of my valley chest,

lay on me soft like a secret,
hiding things that want to be true,
and when we twirl, when we twirl,
dash out like the stones skim the lake.

Notes

"The Lessons" and "Ode to the Sword Logic" are inspired by Oryx and the Sword Logic from Bungie's *Destiny* canon. "The Lessons" and "Ode to the Sword Logic" also owe a creative debt to the work *Kill Six Billion Demons* by Tom Parkinson-Morgan and his concept of Royalty.

"A poem breaks" and "The First Dress" owe a creative debt to the work of Claire Heinzerling.

"My Father Comes Back From The War" owes a creative debt to *Hall of Waters* by Camellia Berry Grass.

"Duplex (A poem breaks where it has to)" is a duplex, a form invented by Jericho Brown.

"The Book of Eve" respectfully draws inspiration from the work of Rabbi Isaac ben Solomon Luria Ashkenazi.

"Solstice" and "In Your Father's House" take their form from Kaveh Akbar's poem "Pilgrim Bell" from his book of the same title.

"The End of Time" is written after "The End of Poetry" by Ada Limón.

Thank You

Much gratitude to Sundress Publications for publishing this book and believing in it.

Thank you so much to my editor, Erin Elizabeth Smith, for your diligence and eyes on this book.

Thank you so much to Kit and Pibob for continuing to believe in my work while I wrestled with it, and for believing in me when I wrestled with myself. Thank you infinitely for your unfaltering friendship and support over the years. I could not do this work without your care.

Thank you to Hannah for your eyes, your ears, your heart, your faith, your unyielding kindness. I could not be who I am without your support. I owe so much to you. Words here cannot communicate enough my appreciation for you. I love you so much.

This book could not exist without the community, care, and craft offered by the following people: Cammy, Rhiannon, Hayley, Maya, Nico, Lye, Mads, Knight, Emmet, Evie, Claire, Shel, Vin, Reuben, Lyn, [Sarah] Cavar, Luther Hughes, Sarah Clark, torrin a greathouse, Mag Gabbert, Milena Bee, and noor ibn najam.

My poetry would not have been able to unfold into the shape it has now without the space made for me by other trans writers who inspired me along the way, including:

torrin a greathouse, MIKA/Coyote/Dagger, Never Angeline Nørth, Porpentine Charity Heartscape, Lip Manegio, Keaton St. James, Paige Lewis, Briar Ripley Page, Franny Choi, Danez Smith, Gerard Way, Mia Nie, Carta

Monir, Remy Boydell, Frog K/Paris Green, Blake Planty, Ava Hofmann, stupid, Imogen Binnie, merritt k, Isabel Fall, Shel Raphen, Jackie Ess, Pibob, Claire Heinzerling, Vin Tanner, [Sarah] Cavar, Ivy Ruth Langley, and Camellia-Berry Grass.

Note on Authorship

Hello, lovely reader. Thank you so much for making it to the end of my book, *Still My Father's Son.* It means so much to me that you would let this book into your heart.

This book was a challenging and at times overwhelming adventure in authenticity and vulnerability. I tried my very hardest to pour my whole self into this book—all aspects of myself, with all of the complexities that entails.

For this reason, I feel it is necessary to add a note at the end of this manuscript. I (we) "identify as" a plural system. What does that mean? While many people experience selfhood as a single, cohesive identity, for many others, ourselves included, identity is a fragmented, segmented, or otherwise pluralized thing. Without euphemism, we are a collective of selves/identities/personalities which share a single body.

This kind of experience has gone through many iterations of nomenclature and pathologization. Historically, this kind of experience has been known by such names as "Multiple Personality Disorder," "Dissociative Identity Disorder," "Other Specified Dissociative Disorder," "Dissociative Disorder Not Otherwise Specified," etc. The valence of these labels is as varied in the community as there are individual perspectives. Personally, while we understand the utility and value of such labels, we choose to identify ourselves first and foremost as "plural," without medicalized or pathologized qualification.

Our plurality is inseparable from our experience in this world as (a) human being(s). We cannot talk about ourselves, our experiences, our traumas and aspirations, without also discussing our plurality. As we share this book with you, this exercise in authenticity, we also wish to share with you an authentic understanding of the process of this book's creation.

Like all books, this book could not have been made without the collective effort of an entire community behind it. Just as there have been individuals and collectives outside of our physical body who have contributed to this book's realization, so have there been individuals and collectives within our physical body who have each contributed to this project in their own ways.

We want to take this time to name and thank the people in our system who have contributed to each part of this project.

We are a group of people who collectively go by the professional name "Nora Hikari." In our intimate social life, we are also known by many other names, including "The Wires System," "Wires," "Mal," "Hikari," and others. It is by these names which we would like to acknowledge our individual contributions to this project.

Within-system editing of this manuscript was completed by Nora Hikari.

The individual pieces in this collection have been authored by:

The River Asks if I am Ready to Die, God Asks if I am Prepared to Survive
By Wires

The Lessons
By Wires and Mal

Notes on a Poem
By Wires

Ode to the Sword Logic
By Wires

Mother (n) - Definition
By Wires

A History of Tongues
By Wires

Sermon
By Wires

A poem breaks
By Wires

The Instructables Guide To Becoming Your Father
By Wires and Mal

The Lessons
By Wires and Mal

Imago Dei
By Wires

The Beloved Ruin
By Wires

My Father Comes Back From The War
By Wires and Mal

In Your Father's House
By Wires

Petitionary
By Wires

Fireflies
By Wires

An incomplete list of things I have not said to my mother about the mail
By Hikari and Wires

The Lessons
By Wires and Mal

Duplex (a poem breaks where it has to)
By Hikari and Wires

Fragments
By Wires

Monologue for Five Selves
By Mal

On Naming
By Wires

Hamartiology, or, the Theological Study of Sin, Changes Her Name To The
First Law Of Thermodynamics
By Hikari and Wires

The End of Time
By Hikari and Wires

Airline Safety Placard (A prayer)
By Hikari and Wires

Love Letter to the Jar of Q-Tips in My Bathroom in Eighth Grade
By Wires

Solstice
By Hikari

Palinode for the Throat
By Hikari

The Body Answers
By Hikari

The Book of Eve
By Hikari

Figure 1.1 (Attractive Forces)
By Hikari

Gardner
By Hikari

Ode to Lampshade
By Hikari

My Heartful Songlikes
By Hikari

Anti-ode to Wholeness
By Hikari and Wires

The Birds
By Hikari

Helpless
By Hikari

Letter
By Hikari and Wires and Mal

The First Dress
By Hikari and Wires

Other Sundress Titles

The Parachutist
Jose Hernandez Diaz
$16

Pure Fear, American Legend
Laura Dzubay
$20

Florence
Bess Cooley
$16

Spoke the Dark Matter
Michelle Whittaker
$16

DANGEROUS BODIES/ANGER ODES
stevie redwood
$16

Back to Alabama
Valerie A. Smith
$16

Good Son
Kyle Liang
$16

Grief Slut
Evelyn Berry
$16

Slaughterhouse for Old Wives Tales
Hannah V Warren
$16

Ruin & Want
José Angel Araguz
$20

Nocturne in Joy
Tatiana Johnson-Boria
$16

Age of Forgiveness
Caleb Curtiss
$16

Another Word for Hunger
Heather Bartlett
$16

Where My Umbilical is Buried
Amanda Galvan-Huynh
$16

Little Houses
Athena Nassar
$16

www.ingramcontent.com/pod-product-compliance
Lightning Source LLC
Chambersburg PA
CBHW021509090426
42739CB00007B/544